# Tasty TRAVELS

Glenn Cosby

OXFORD
UNIVERSITY PRESS

CW00953882

# OXFORD
## UNIVERSITY PRESS

Great Clarendon Street, Oxford, OX2 6DP, United Kingdom

Oxford University Press is a department of the University
of Oxford. It furthers the University's objective of excellence
in research, scholarship, and education by publishing
worldwide. Oxford is a registered trade mark of Oxford
University Press in the UK and in certain other countries

British Library Cataloguing in Publication Data
Data available

ISBN: 978-0-19-830827-0

10 9 8 7 6 5 4 3 2 1

Paper used in the production of this book is a natural, recyclable
product made from wood grown in sustainable forests. The
manufacturing process conforms to the environmental
regulations of the country of origin.

Printed in China by Hing Yip

## Acknowledgements

Series Editor: Nikki Gamble
Illustrations: Kate Rochester
Photography: Studio 8

The publisher would like to thank the following for permission
to reproduce photographs: **p4**: Paul Rich Studio/Shutterstock;
**p5**: Kesu/Shutterstock; **p10**: Lilyana Vynogradova/Shutterstock;
**p11**: nito/Shutterstock; **p12**: Joe Gough/Shutterstock; **p16**: Kelvin
Wong/Shutterstock; **p19**: Peter Zijlstra/Shutterstock

UK

France

Spain

Jamaica

# Contents

| | |
|---|---|
| Introduction | 4 |
| France | 6 |
| Spain | 10 |
| India | 12 |
| Australia | 16 |
| Jamaica | 18 |
| The UK | 22 |
| Glossary | 24 |

**India**

**Australia**

# Introduction

Hello, I'm Glenn. I took part in *The Great British Bake Off*, a baking competition that was shown on television in the UK.

I have always loved food. My earliest memory is the smell of my nan's fish and chips, made with freshly caught fish. She also made the best cakes and pies, and she taught me how to bake.

I love making cakes but there's more to me than baking! I also love all types of food from around the world.

I am from Bedford, UK, which has a mix of people from different places like Italy, Pakistan, the Caribbean and Poland. I grew up eating wonderful food from lots of different countries.

As a child, I used to love going to friends' houses and being offered crispy delicious pizza or golden lentil soup. Every family has their own favourites. If someone offers you something you've never eaten before, give it a try!

When I was little, we went on holiday to France and I have loved travelling ever since. Each place is different but there are always interesting people and there is always amazing food.

# France

My first holiday ever was at a campsite by the sea in France. On the way back from the beach, we bought sweet, juicy fruit to eat.

For a special treat we had thin pancakes called crêpes. We watched them being made in the crêpe van and sometimes ate them with fruit.

6

It is nice to have something sweet for dessert and fruit is the perfect healthy choice. Fruit contains lots of **vitamins**, **minerals** and **fibre**.

### Fresh is best

Some types of fruit are nice all year round. But there's nothing better than the taste of a freshly picked peach that has ripened in the summer sun.

# Crêpes with fruit
## Serves 6

### Ingredients

the juice of half a lemon

15 g (grams) icing sugar

300 g fresh fruit, washed

250 g plain flour

a pinch of salt

2 eggs

600 ml (millilitres) of milk

a little sunflower oil

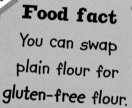

**Food fact**
You can swap plain flour for gluten-free flour.

Always wash your hands with soap before you start to cook.

**Ask an adult for help.**

1. Mix the lemon juice and icing sugar in a bowl.

2. Slice the fruit into the lemon juice mix.

3. Put the flour and salt into another bowl and crack the eggs on top.

4. Add the milk a little at a time, whisking the ingredients together to make batter.

5. Use some scrunched-up kitchen paper to wipe a small frying pan with a little sunflower oil. Put the pan over a medium heat for 1 minute.

6. Use a ladle to pour in some batter and then tilt the pan so the batter spreads out.

7. Cook the crêpe until bubbles appear and the edges go brown, then flip the crêpe over with a spatula (or toss it if you feel brave!) and cook the other side for 2–3 minutes.

8. Put the crêpe onto a plate. Spoon some of the fruit mixture in a line along the centre of the crêpe and roll it up.

**Food fact**

You can swap the fruit mixture for cheese, meat or vegetables.

# Spain

My happiest memories of Spain are from when I lived in a city called Barcelona. Every **region** of Spain has its own special dishes. My favourite is the simplest – instead of using butter, you smear your bread with soft, ripe tomatoes. Wonderful!

### Food fact

It is important to eat plenty of fruit and vegetables. They give our bodies the vitamins and minerals we need to stay healthy.

Spanish food changes through the year as the weather changes.

In summer, when it's hotter, many fruits are at their best.

In winter and spring, people eat more vegetables, such as grilled **calçots** (*say* kal-sots) which taste a lot like leeks. They are cooked on a grill and served with a sauce made from peppers and almonds. You eat them with your fingers – yummy but messy!

**Food fact**

As people move around the world, they take their favourite foods with them. People from North Africa moved to Spain hundreds of years ago and brought foods such as rice, almonds and dates.

## India

When I was 19, I travelled around India by train. I can remember the sound of people shouting, "Tea, tea?" and the hot spicy smell of the food as the trains pulled into the station.

As passengers got on and off, people sold food and drinks through the train windows. I enjoyed eating vegetable snacks called pakoras (*say* pa-kor-uz).

### Food fact

In India, lots of people are vegetarians, so there are many foods that are made from vegetables and healthy **pulses** such as lentils. Foods like lentil dhal (*say* d-ar-l) are simple and delicious!

**Food fact**
Pulses are a great way for vegetarians to get protein. Our bodies need protein to grow and repair themselves.

13

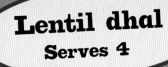

# Lentil dhal
## Serves 4

**Ingredients**

250 g split red lentils

1 teaspoon of turmeric

1 stock cube

1 litre of water

a knob of butter

1 small onion

1 clove of garlic

1 teaspoon of ground cumin

LENTILS

1. Put the lentils in a large saucepan with the turmeric, the stock cube and the water.

2. Boil gently over a medium heat for 20 minutes, stirring occasionally, until the lentils are soft and the water has been **absorbed**.

3. While the lentils are cooking, melt the butter in a frying pan.

4. Carefully slice the onion and garlic and add them to the pan.

5. Fry the onions and garlic over a medium heat until they are golden brown, then add the cumin and fry for 3 minutes.

6. Combine the onions and garlic with the lentils and serve.

# Australia

I lived in Australia for a year and travelled all over the enormous country. Australians and New Zealanders have traditional dishes like **pavlova** which is now eaten all over the world.

The weather in Australia made my Christmas traditions seem strange. I remember having a barbecue on the beach on Christmas Day and singing songs about a snowy Christmas. Christmas is during the summer in Australia so there was no chance of snow at all!

## Farming in Australia

**Aboriginal people** have lived in Australia for thousands of years. Traditionally, they hunted animals such as kangaroos. They also searched for food such as seeds, vegetables and fruit. Some Aboriginal people still do this today.

**European people** started moving to Australia in the eighteenth century. They brought plants and animals with them and people in Australia started to grow crops such as wheat.

17

# Jamaica

There are many other places that I want to travel to. One place that I am keen to visit is Jamaica in the Caribbean. The Caribbean islands have a wonderful variety of people and foods.

I used to be a teacher in London and in one of the schools, all of the cooks came from the Caribbean. They often served exotic spicy foods like **jerk chicken** and goat curry. One day I hope to go to Jamaica and taste these lovely foods again.

**Food fact**
Chicken is a good source of protein. Our bodies need protein to grow.

**Food fact**
Plantains look like sweet bananas but they are savoury and are usually cooked before being eaten. They can be boiled, baked or fried.

## Jerk chicken
### Serves 6

### Ingredients

1 tablespoon of sunflower oil

1 kg (kilogram) chicken thighs

100 g jerk paste

1 can of kidney beans

100 ml of water

1 can of coconut milk

200 g long grain rice

1 teaspoon of salt

**Food fact**

Sunflower oil is a type of fat. Fats are an important part of a balanced diet but it is easy to have too much fat.

**Food fact**

Rice is a grain. Grains contain carbohydrates, another important part of a healthy diet. Carbohydrates give us lots of energy.

1. Heat the oven to 180°C (gas mark 4).

2. Heat the oil in a roasting tin, then carefully add the chicken pieces and roast them in the oven for 10 minutes.

3. Use a spoon to coat each piece of chicken with jerk paste.

Ask an adult for help.

4. Put the chicken back into the oven and roast it for 45 minutes.

5. While the chicken is roasting, pour the kidney beans into a sieve over a large pan, collecting the juice in the pan.

6. Add the water, coconut milk, rice and salt to the juice from the beans and then **simmer** on the hob for 10 minutes. Add the beans then put the lid on the pan and cook for another 10 minutes.

7. Drain and serve straight away with the roast chicken.

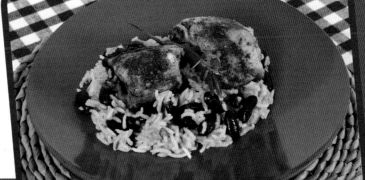

# The UK

I love travelling but there's no place like home. I live by the sea in Devon in the UK. One of my favourite things to do in the winter is to take my dog for a walk on the beach.

After some exercise in the cold air, I have a traditional Devon cream tea – scones with jam and **clotted cream**, and a warm cup of tea.

## Scones
### Makes about 10

**Ingredients**

50 g softened salted butter (plus extra for greasing)

350 g plain flour (plus extra for dusting)

2 eggs

100 ml of milk

50 g sugar

2 teaspoons of baking powder

**Food fact**

It's OK to eat some sugar but too much is unhealthy and can damage our teeth.

Ask an adult for help.

1. Heat the oven to 200°C (gas mark 6) and lightly grease a baking tray.

2. Put the flour and butter into a bowl. Rub the butter into the flour by pressing it between your fingers and thumbs.

3. Crack the eggs into a jug, add the milk and whisk them together.

4. Set aside 1 tablespoon of the egg mixture. Pour the rest into the flour.

5. Add the sugar and baking powder and mix the dough into a ball with your hands.

6. Dust the table with flour and put the dough onto the table. Dust the top of the dough with flour and roll it until it is 2 cm thick.

7. Cut the dough into circles and put them on the baking tray. Brush the remaining egg mixture over the top of each one.

8. Bake in the oven for 10 minutes.

# Glossary

**Aboriginal people:** people who originally lived in Australia before European people arrived

**absorbed:** soaked up

**calçots:** a type of green onions that are grown in Spain

**°C:** short for degrees Celsius, we use it to measure how hot or cold something is

**carbohydrates:** substances that give us energy and are found in foods such as grains, pulses and potatoes

**clotted cream:** extra thick cream

**dhal:** a type of food made with pulses

**European people:** people who come from a country in Europe

**fats:** substances in foods such as dairy products that provide energy which can be stored. Some foods, such as oily fish, contain healthy fats.

**fibre:** a substance that helps our body to digest our food

**gluten-free:** food that is made without gluten, which is found in wheat, barley and rye

**jerk chicken:** spicy cooked chicken

**minerals:** natural substances like calcium and potassium which our bodies need to stay healthy

**pavlova:** a dessert made from meringue and usually topped with cream and fruit

**protein:** a substance found in meat, fish, eggs and pulses; protein helps our body grow and repair itself

**pulses:** foods like beans, lentils and peas which are the seeds of certain plants

**region:** part of a country

**simmer:** boil gently over a low heat

**vegetarians:** people who do not eat meat

**vitamins:** natural substances, often found in fruit and vegetables, that help our bodies to stay healthy